TRANS METRO-POLITAN:

LONELY CITY

TRANS-METRO-POLITAN:

LONELY CITY

Warren_Ellis

Writer

Darick_Robertson

Penciller

Rodney_Ramos
Inker

Nathan_Eyring
Colorist

Clem_Robins
Letterer

Jim Lee (#25-27)
Tony Harris and Ray Snyder (#28)
Tony Harris and Jim Royal (#29)
Tony Harris and Drew Geraci (#30)
Original Series Covers

TRANSMETROPOLITAN created by
Warren_Ellis and Darick_Robertson

Karen Berger SVP – Executive Editor Stuart Moore Cliff Chiang Editors – Original Series
Georg Brewer VP – Design & DC Direct Creative Bob Harras Group Editor – Collected Editions
Scott Nybakken Editor Robbin Brosterman Design Director – Books Curtis King Senior Art Director

DC COMICS

Paul Levitz President & Publisher Richard Bruning SVP – Creative Director Patrick Caldon EVP – Finance & Operations
Amy Genkins SVP – Business & Legal Affairs Jim Lee Editorial Director – WildStorm Gregory Noveck SVP – Creative Affairs
Steve Rotterdam SVP – Sales & Marketing Cheryl Rubin SVP – Brand Management

Cover art by Jim Lee.

TRANSMETROPOLITAN: LONELY CITY

Published by DC Comics. Cover and compilation Copyright © 2009 DC Comics. All Rights Reserved.

DC Comics, 1700 Broadway, New York, NY 10019. A Warner Bros. Entertainment Company. Printed in Canada. First Printing.
ISBN: 978-1-4012-2819-4

INTRODUCTION

Warren Ellis asked me to write this and I am O.K. with that up to a point. My unease is that the point is unnervingly sharp and very likely to turn in my direction. Here is the problem. Warren knows that I am a TRANSMETROPOLITAN fan, but how can he expect me to write about that? Does he think I just came down the Clyde on a tea biscuit? No sirree, this is not my first barbecue. If I write that Spider Jerusalem is my hero, does he think Spider will let me get away with that? I would be lucky to only suffer a blast from a bowel disrupter and it is much more likely my eyeballs will be popped as easily as squeezing a pustule and fed to the cat. If I write that TRANSMET is a beacon of brilliant irony and sardonic satire could I survive the torrent of saliva-drenched invective and scorn S.J. would heap on me? If I wrote that TRANSMET made me laugh like a drain are there enough lavatory bowls to contain Jerusalem's vomit? If I confessed that I lusted after the filthy assistants what foul perversions would I be accused of? If I praised the artwork as the wittiest, most disturbing since George Grosz I would soon find myself depicted as a fucked-up, mechanics-addicted, feces-smeared background character. If I hailed this vision of the future as persuasive and properly terrifying I might never live to see it. You get my problem?

I think, however, that I can safely say this: I know this City, I have read The Word, I have listened to these politicians, I have smelt the stink of greed, I have thrown stuff at the TV, I have wondered what future there is for Truth and Beauty. I have wanted to go and live on the top of a Yorkshire moor.

Warren, tell Spider to stay healthy and keep writing the column.

— Patrick Stewart

Patrick Stewart's accomplishments on stage and screen are legion, but he is perhaps best known for his acclaimed one-man performance of Charles Dickens' A Christmas Carol *and his ongoing role as Captain Jean-Luc Picard in the* Star Trek: The Next Generation *television and film series.*

WARREN ELLIS writes &
DARICK ROBERTSON pencils

HERE TO GO

RODNEY RAMOS - inker   CLEM ROBINS - letterer   NATHAN EYRING - color & separations
JIM LEE - cover   CLIFF CHIANG - assistant editor   STUART MOORE - editor
TRANSMETROPOLITAN created by Warren Ellis & Darick Robertson

...AN UNSETTLING MOMENT AT THE PRESIDENTIAL INAUGURATION WHEN THE NEW PRESIDENT APPEARED TO SPEAK IN TONGUES FOR A FULL MINUTE; "JUST A COUGH," SAYS ADVISOR SCHACT...

...ON CURRENT MOVEMENTS, THE RAIN FALLING ON CENTRAL AND WESTERN AREAS OF THE CITY IS PREDICTED TO CEASE IN NINE MINUTES...

...ENGLISH AUTHOR DECLARES U.S. "CULTURE OF VICTIMS"; BEATEN TO DEATH BY CROWD, PARTICIPANTS SUE AUTHOR'S FAMILY FOR DAMAGE INCURRED TO KNUCKLES, FINGERNAILS...

I love the City in the rain.

GUY'S

TESTICLES

DELIVERIES IN THE REAR

GUY'S

The last of the spring rains is here; soft, on light wind, the sort of spring breeze that ruffles your hair like a playful sister.

If you've got hair.

People on the streets stop, now, to open their mouths, drink it down, cold and clean and fresh.

We'd hide from it, cover our faces as if we were facing a firestorm; like some bastard God was pissing acid on us.

Couldn't do that when I was a kid. The rain was poison.

NOT THAT I'D BLAME HIM.

Now, I watch it running over girls' chins, making their skin glisten like pure and elegantly worked crystal...

...down on the street, phoneports, sidewalkscreens and road control arches are made new again by the water...

...and children lead wonderfully unbelieving old women by the hand into the rain...

I REMEMBER FIRST LEARNING ABOUT DEATH QUITE VIVIDLY.

COULDN'T HELP MYSELF.

IT WAS TERRIBLE, REALLY.

DAD WAS DRIVING A BUS FOR A LIVING, THE RUN FROM THE DOCKS TO THE FAR TERMINUS OF THE FOURTH CANAL.

MOO HOO HA HA.

HIS SHIFT FINISHED ABOUT THE SAME TIME SCHOOL GOT OUT, SO SOMETIMES I'D WALK DOWN TO THE BUS DEPOT TO MEET HIM FOR A RIDE HOME.

ONE DAY I GET THERE AND SEE MAD RADHU GUMBEER BEING LED OUT OF THE DEPOT IN TEARS.

Mad Radhu Gumbeer was the man who drove the Bedford-Handsworth run. The only man who drove the Bedford-Handsworth run.

MAD RADHU GUMBEER WAS A ONE-MAN ARSENAL, THE MAN WHO COULD REDUCE YOU TO A SMEAR OF PROTEIN EVEN WHEN--HEY!

--EVEN WHEN STRIPPED NAKED AND MISSING HIS ENTIRE TOP THREE LAYERS OF SKIN.

17

SEAN, COLM, SHERLOCK, AND THE OTHER ONE: THE **BRADY BROTHERS** RESTING IN PEACE INSIDE THE CANISTER THEIR JOINT REMAINS WERE SCRAPED INTO

Which was, indeed, how he killed the Butchers of Spring Corner when they ambushed his bus, robbed all the passengers, and tortured him for the code to the on-bus fare safe.

HE DROPPED ACID BOMBS FROM LITTLE HATCHES IN THE BASE OF HIS TESTICLES, PISSED DISSEMBLER ALL OVER THEM, BLINDED THEM WITH ORGAN-SPECIFIC TOXINS SPRAYED FROM HIS NIPPLES.

--AND CLAIMED HE DID IT ALL FOR THE VIRGIN MARY--

WHO, HE SAID, LIVED DOWN HIS STREET AND WORE INDIAN ARMY BOOTS.

HE WAS MY HERO.

AND HERE HE WAS, THE SINGLE HARDEST AND MOST FRIGHTENING MAN I'D EVER KNOWN--THE ONLY ADULT I TRULY RESPECTED--CRYING LIKE A BABY.

I COULDN'T HELP IT. I ASKED HIM WHAT WAS WRONG.

I SQUASHED A NUN.

18

HE TOOK THE CORNER AT SUSTER'S END, SMOOTH AND CONTROLLED AS USUAL, THINKING ABOUT THE GUN EMPLACEMENTS FACING HIM UP THE ROAD AT WILKES BOOTH FIELD, LOOKING AHEAD...

AND ON THE RIGHT, THIS GODDAMN NUN--

--PEDALING AWAY ON HER PUSH-BIKE, JUST BLISSFULLY SINGING AND FLAPPING AND OBVIOUSLY TRUSTING TO GOD TO KEEP HER SAFE SO'S SHE DOESN'T HAVE TO BOTHER LOOKING WHERE SHE'S FUCKING GOING--

--SHOOTS STRAIGHT UNDER THE WHEELS OF THE BUS,

AND THE LAST THING HE SEES OF HER --I SWEAR IT'S TRUE--

MAD RAGHU

BUS

BIG DON'S MEAT CO

PRESHUSH

MANNY'S PLATFORM 5

5 MANNY'S

WELCOME

WHAT? YOU WANT TO HEAR SOMETHING DISGUSTING?

FUCKING VULTURES.

ALL RIGHT, I'VE GOT ONE FOR YOU.

SHE'S EIGHT-EEN YEARS OLD, SHE'S BEAUTIFUL, SHE'S SMART, SHE'S A DANCER, SHE'S ESSENTIALLY GODDAMN PERFECT, AND SHE SPENDS EVERY DAY TRYING TO TAMP DOWN HYSTERICAL TERROR.

EVERY FUCKING DAY.

SHE MISSES HER BROTHER.

HER BROTHER WAS KIND TO HER, YOU SEE?

HER MOTHER WAS A MAD RELIGIOUS DOMESTIC TERRORIST WHO RULED BY GUILT AND FEAR, HER ELDEST BROTHER WAS A HALF-BRIGHT THING WELL ON THE WAY TO VIOLENT MONSTERDOM, AND HER FATHER WAS A GHOST IN AN ARMCHAIR, SILENT AND INSUBSTANTIAL.

BUT HER OTHER BROTHER, ALSO OLDER THAN HER-- HE WAS KIND.

ONE DAY, THE KIDS FROM THE HOUSING PROJECT WHERE THEY YANK MUTATED FROGS OUT OF THE SEWAGE FLOW AND FUCK 'EM WERE THROWING ROCKS AT HER.

THAT HOUSING PROJECT STILL THERE, YOU KNOW. MILLENNIUM DIP, NORTH EAST. APPARENTLY THE FROGS EXPLODE ON YO DICK AT THE MOMENT OF ORGASM.

WARREN ELLIS writes & **DARICK ROBERTSON** pencils

21 DAYS IN THE CITY

RODNEY RAMOS - inker   **CLEM ROBINS** - letterer   **NATHAN EYRING** - color & separations

JIM LEE - cover art   **CLIFF CHIANG** - assistant editor   **STUART MOORE** - editor

TRANSMETROPOLITAN created by Warren Ellis & Darick Robertson

My name's Spider Jerusalem. I am the most beloved man in this City. I am a journalist. I write a column for a newspaper called THE WORD entitled I HATE IT HERE. Because I do. I hate it and I hate you. And you love me for it. That's the way it works. And if you argue with the way it works, I'll kick off the top of your head and shit on your living brain. And you will love me for it.

Thank God for me.

The City changes its makeup. Its foundation's gone scabby, lipstick kissed off, mascara run down its face. Down come the Beast's colors, all grey and doomed, their bite and bluster all dried up and blown down rustling autumn streets. And everywhere, blooming, The Smiler's colors, a blaze of victory bouquets all across the City.

First he fucks the City, then he buys her a new dress. Lovely. Maybe we should count ourselves lucky he didn't just wipe his dick on our knee and toss five bucks onto the bed.

 in charge

TOUGH MAN, TOUGH LUCK.

LOSER

BYE BYE BEAS

She hasn't brushed her hair. His hair is still dewy with droplets from the shower. Their eyes, too used to half-light, get half burned out by the sunshine. They groan, lean on each other and laugh at themselves. Share his last cigarette in front of the hotel, waiting for a cab, or perhaps two.

I spent last night sniffling cat urine. The cat pissed in some mystery cesspool she keeps somewhere in the apartment, that I've yet to locate. I lay there, cat urine festering in my twitching nostrils, listening to both my assistants having sex with near-brain-dead teenagers they'd picked up at some retard bar over in West Egg. For nine hours and twenty-seven minutes.

"I'm doing mechanics," he says, fingers tapping in unconscious urgency on the sharp edges of a credit-card-sized AI computer brain; same kind of servant-mind you find in your Maker, one that comes with the standard chemical scanning gear that checks your food as fit for consumption. Some bastard here's selling mechanics, and he wants some. Not needs. Not yet. Mechanics is – at least begins as – a drug, one new enough that we haven't yet developed addiction resistance to it. A drug whose chemical code is also machine code. Make the AI card scan the drug, do the drug yourself, and you and the machine intelligence both get good and fucked up. The drug creates a connection between your mind and the AI. The AI breaks into your head and starts messing around with your DNA. Move a human chemical here, juggle some more there – and human tissue becomes mineral matter. You grow mechanics. The high passes. The mechanics remain.

MADE

THE SUCKING CONTINUES

WARNING:
THIS BENCH BECOMES
RED HOT BETWEEN
1 A.M. & 7 A.M.
NO SLEEPING

35

Matteo bought himself a new set of genitals today. He's very proud of them. They were made by an Uraguayan firm known for the reliability and sensitivity of their product. They're also known for having their products built by children working in dangerous conditions earning less than a dollar a month, but that doesn't bother Matteo. Oh no. Matteo's got the genitals he always wanted now. They're exactly like the genitals he used to have. Only with a MiniDisc player.

Sometimes this place just stops and hits you in the eyes. I'm on a train to Venetian End to cover the intestine-rinsing competition at the public sinks there, passing through the western Lakes. Sunny day. Trout and salmon blasting through the channels and rivers that connect the Lakes to each other and the sea. And then I see a dolphin. And then I see a Temp, someone wearing animal traits for a weekend. And for a moment there, I don't have any words.

And when the sun falls down on this City, it's transformed; it blooms again, in impossible blazes of a million colors you'd forgotten even existed, winter's been here so long. It wakes me, shakes me from the grey I'd been living in, reminds me why I'm alive, why I'm here, why I do what I do. My filthy assistants disagree and I have to force them blinking and cursing into the light, as if prodding them into walking the plank. Which thought also warms me as if the sun were in my belly.

My editor, Mitchell Royce, makes me attend a Media Exploitation meeting at the offices of THE WORD, the crapulous rag you currently have slowly dissolving in your hands. It does not go well. I am shown Magical Truthsaying Bastard Spidey, animated versions of my columns in the manner of Japanese cartoons. I am shown enough useless shit to make shelters for every war refugee in western England. I am forced to remonstrate physically with the media rep, until Royce stuns me with wads of royalty money.

Right Love is somehow becoming a cause célèbre among the great and the good. Huey Three-Flint-Knife, their founder and spokesman, is handsome, witty and impassioned. His friends, like Bobby Long, plainly worship him – Long spent his two years in jail writing a history of the movement that was nothing more than a hymn to Huey. Influential producer and cultural compass Bert Shenfield said upon meeting him, "If he's not Mao, I'll eat it." Please allow me to remind everyone that Right Love's aim of "freeing sexuality" is quite specific: having sex with pre-sexual humans. Don't look for media-approved ideologically sound Right Causes where there are none. Look out of the window instead, and do something about what you see there.

VICTIM # 50432

40

My dreams come true. A strain of intelligent sociopathic dog has arisen in the dank sewers of Hilbery Depth, northeast of the Fourth Canal terminus. These criminal vermin have terrorized the decent people there so badly, and have bred so prodigiously, that Civic Center is permitting, for only the third time in living memory, a Cull. Smart or not, dogs have no rights. I ponder this awful, searing injustice as I fondle my Volunteer Cullmaster pass and assemble my arsenal.

Sometimes, life is sweet.

I grew up here, during its worst years. Fresh crocodile shit piled against front doors, steaming in the dockland chill. It was never warm here. Never. Mom picking up fat dock lizards, dashing their brains out on Dad and throwing them on the fire, watching them blacken and split and catch, squirting hot fat out of the hearth. Spending days and nights sitting out on the sidewalk with the other kids, listening to all our parents spouting uneducated hate-filled bullshit over cheap beers and thinking, is this it? and is that me in twenty years? and planning our escapes, from eight years old planning our grand escapes from our lives

Whenever I come back here, I wonder who got out.

I love shopping. No, really. Nothing pleases me more than wandering through a good market's aisles, my gun tapping musically on the cart's steel, stun grenades bumping my leg companionably. Spiced seahorses in brine, fresh chimp heads on ice along with the salmon, manatee and whale … powdered children from Ireland mixed up in a jug of vodka for those summer days on the balcony … what a time to be alive, when delicacies from all over the world, some only half-imagined, are there to be had on a nearby shelf…

I had one of those weird crossed lines the other day, the ones that connect you to Mars. I'm guessing it's something to do with the revolutionary faction on Pylon Nine, whom most people are certain are only rebelling because they feel they really ought to. It's a cultural expectation. I ended up having phone sex with a nominal female who had a sequence of filtration pipes, vacuum seals and musical valves instead of a mouth. She sent me a picture later, though, and she had pretty lips. I'm oddly depressed.

Listened to filthy assistants having wild fantasy steroid monkey sex again last night.

I live behind a wall so high it gets more difficult each day to see over it. When I first returned to the streets of the City, I was put in a hopeless shithole. Once I'd made the Word some money, I got them to move me to Pupin Grove, which was nicer, if filled with people who were something-in-media. That place turned out to be insecure, and I was moved to expensive, safe Chase Square. And when I broke the Josh Freeh story, they set me up in ultra-exclusive Puritan Mews here. And now I can't see the street anymore.

Did you ever want to set someone's head on fire, just to see what it looked like? Did you ever stand in the street and think to yourself, I could make that nun go blind just by giving her a kiss? Did you ever lay out plans for stitching babies and stray cats into a Perfect New Human? Did you ever stand naked surrounded by people who want your gleaming sperm, squirting frankincense, soma and testosterone from every pore? If so, then you're the bastard who stole my drugs Friday night. And I'll find you. Oh, yes.

Sumo is the most perfect of sports. It has elegance, ceremony, danger, art, speed, and, most important, two fat bastards smacking the shit out of each other. It is immaculate, which is why it has remained essentially unchanged for thousands of years. It remains the only thing in the world that I want to see stay static.
The only thing I love that loves me back.

He met God in t
night, walking
his hotel in t
rain, like he w
written
Hemingway, steppi
slowly through
place where nurs
die if you kiss th
and syphilis stea
your friends t
minute you lo
away. God stopp
and talked to h
for a while, qui
solemn words in t
heart of the dar
And then
Essential Stre
Station God sat do
and wept. He – t
kid who told me th
– suffers from t
naiveté trait th
parents thought we
cute twenty yea
ago. He has a pr
civilization neur
connectivity. Whe
we have instin
that, no, y
shouldn't cross t
road,
hallucinates G
telling him not
cross the road. I'
heard that naive
trait is getti
trendy again.
you're thinkin
about it, thi
about the b
weeping uncontro
lably as God cri
for him not
cross t
stree

I'VE GOT A DATA MINER RUNNING. IT'S COMPARING MISSING PERSONS AGAINST PERSONALITY TRAITS AND DOMESTIC SITUATIONS. THE PERSON WHO KILLED VITA SEVERN WAS SO THOROUGHLY VAPORIZED THAT NO EVIDENCE WHATSOEVER REMAINED, APART FROM THE GUN, WHICH WAS SANITIZED. ONCE I'VE GOT A SPREAD OF NAMES, I CAN HAVE QUESTIONS ASKED. I CAN COVER THE STORY. NO ONE'S GETTING AWAY WITH THIS. THE NEW PRESIDENT HAS PROMISED TO FUCK ME OVER. BUT IF I CAN MANAGE THIS, I CAN GET HIM FIRST. IF.

I'VE BEEN GETTING HEADACHES LATELY.

(NOT FOR PUBLICATION.)

The internal strife in Ludgate East finally burned itself out a couple of years back. Everyone thought the bombed-out district would just rot, since there was no way Civic Center were going to send cash. No one figured on the assholes, though. The tourist assholes come for a holiday in someone else's misery, in their retro-Vietcong black pajamas and urban camo dresses, here to see what an actual war looks like. And the rebels smile and say Hi, I'm Marcellus XXX, I'll be your guide for today, selling toy ramcars made from spent shells…

So this corp wants to show me they love me like unto a god by giving me a new forfuck'ssake television set. Approximedia, they called it. Rider signals on the regular digital feed talk to a small Maker inside the set, which pumps out olfactory mix and forcefeed waves. You can see TV, hear it, and now smell it, taste it and feel it.

I am sad to report that it will not be a hit. And that applying it to remastered old films was not clever. Despite the possibilities, I found myself groped by Vincent Price, forced to taste Divine, and attacked by the special scent of several unwashed porn stars being intimate with donkeys. And my filthy assistants were all licked by Warren Oates.

Terrible goddamn place. Some days it's like some bastard nailed a ticket for the bus tour down to fucking Hell to the front of my brain. For every wild everything-depends-on-it first-week-of-being-madly-in-love kiss on a streetcorner, for every beautiful woman stopping to feel the sun on her face and every child dancing in clean rain, there's a kid living in its own shit in a dumpster somewhere while Daddy sells his ass for milk money, tanks breaking down unwanted houses just to stop homeless people squatting there … Time was this place didn't make sense and I could live with it. Either it's changed, or I have.

There's all the good things on this ticket, and pure fucking evil too. And all the same, I'm going down with you.

WARREN ELLIS writes and DARICK ROBERTSON pencils

MONSTERING!

RODNEY RAMOS - inker   CLEM ROBINS - letterer   NATHAN EYRING - color and separations

JIM LEE, cover artist   CLIFF CHIANG - ass't editor   STUART MOORE - editor   TRANSMETROPOLITAN created by WARREN ELLIS and DARICK ROBERTSON

JESUS CHRIST...OWWW... WHICH ONE DID WE FALL ASLEEP DURING?

YOU PASSED OUT DURING "ONCE IN BLOODY ENGLAND." I MADE IT TO THE END OF "DIE, BASTARD VICAR, DIE."

DON'T KNOW HOW YOU SAT THROUGH "BIG COLD LONDON GUNMAN," MYSELF.

GOING FOR A SHOWER.

GOING FOR A SHIT.

TELEVISION! INFORM ME!

PURITAN MEWS DATA FILTERING PRESENTS: SPIDER'S PERSONAL HOTMENU! ABUSE! VIOLENCE! LIES! THEFT! PEOPLE HAVING SEX!

PURITAN MEWS DATA FILTERING

01 02 03 04 06 07 08 09

SPKF TV

WELCOME AND GOOD DAY SPIDER JERUSALEM! SENATOR SWEENEY SCANDAL PURITAN MEWS

search access

THIS MORNING: ESKIMO WINTER IMMIGRANT DIES IN POLICE CUSTODY; DERANGED ARTIFICIAL PENISES LOOSE IN WATER SUPPLY; CITY SENATOR IN CASH/PORN/ CORRUPTION STORM--

"SENATOR."

GOOD MORNING, GOOD MORNING...

I HAVE A PREPARED STATEMENT ON THESE ALLEGATIONS IF YOU'D KINDLY AND QUIETLY LEND ME YOUR EAR...

LADIES AND GENTLEMEN OF THE PRESS: TO ADDRESS EACH AND EVERY ONE OF THESE BASELESS ACCUSATIONS WOULD WASTE BOTH MY TIME AND YOURS.

I HAVE SERVED MY PEOPLE IN CONGRESS AS WELL AS I COULD FOR FIFTEEN YEARS. ONLY NOW, WITH MY PARTY BACK IN POWER, DO PEOPLE SEEK TO--

MISTER SWEENEY!

ANY RESPONSES FROM THE PRESS SHOULD IDEALLY GO TO MY OFFICE, OR MY SECRETARY SYSTEM AT AMFEED SENATOR TARLETON SWEENEY...

CITY • VISION

Sweeney Performs
in Porn Film *maybe*

JERUSALEM

IT BEGINS.

WHAT NEXT?

OH, WE HAVE TO CRANK THIS UP TO WAGNERIAN PROPORTIONS, CHANNON.

THIS ENTIRE CITY IS BAYING FOR HIS *PRICK*, FOR GOD'S SAKE! HOW MUCH WORSE CAN WE MAKE IT?

OKAY, FORGET I SAID ANYTHING STUPID QUESTION.

WHAT'S THE NEXT STEP IN DESTROYING THE POOR FUCKER'S LIFE?

I DON'T SEE WHY ON THE WORST DAY OF MY PROFESSIONAL LIFE MY DAUGHTER COULDN'T DO ME THE FAVOR OF GETTING HER GENOME RESET.

KISS MY GREY ASS, DADDY.

SENATOR SWEENEY, YOUR DAUGHTER'S THE LEAST OF OUR CONCERNS. NOW ABOUT THIS TV SPOT--

IT'S *NOT* THE LEAST OF MY CONCERNS. I'M TOLD TO GO ON TV WITH MY FAMILY TO PLEAD INNOCENCE AND MY DAUGHTER TELLS ME SHE GREW A BACKUP VAGINAL ORIFICE THIS MORNING--

WANNA SEE IT, DADDY? WANNA FILM IT FOR YOUR SICKO PALS?

NOT THAT HE KNOWS WHAT A VAGINAL ORIFICE LOOKS LIKE ANYMORE.

FOR GOD'S SAKE, DEBORAH--

THE RECORD with ROBERT McX

SENATOR SWEENEY, I'D LIKE TO THANK YOU AND YOUR WONDERFUL FAMILY FOR JOINING ME HERE TODAY.

OUR PLEASURE, ROBERT. GLAD TO BE HERE ON THE RECORD, TO SET THE RECORD STRAIGHT.

INDEED.

SO... WHEN DID YOU STOP HAVING SEX WITH YOUR WIFE, AND DOES THIS HAVE ANY BEARING ON YOUR ALLEGED PORN BUSINESS?

ROBERT McX

WHAT NEXT?

SOME ACTUAL JOURNALISM, I THINK.

ACTUAL JOURNALISM? IS THAT WHEN YOU DON'T COMMIT CRIMES?

HELL, NO. IT'S WHEN WE COMMIT REALLY GOOD CRIMES.

MISTER SWEENEY!

YOU CAN'T JUST SHIT ALL OVER THE PRESS, MISTER SWEENEY! WE HAVE QUESTIONS!

WHY DID YOU HOLD UP DEBATE ON THE INTELLIGENT SEXUAL CULTURE SCHEME IN THE SENATE WHEN YOU WERE MAKING PORNO?

MISTER SWEENEY!

COMMUNITY CENTER

BEHOLD!

LOVE JONES

YOU BRING US TO THE NICEST PLACES.

I DON'T BRING YOU ANYWHERE IF I CAN HELP IT. YOU TWO NEVER BEHAVE YOURSELVES IN PUBLIC.

WE DON'T?

SHUT UP.

WHAT ARE WE DOING HERE?

WHAT EVERYONE ELSE SHOULD'VE DONE.

THE SCENE OF THE CRIME.

THIS IS WHERE SWEENEY'S PORNO FILMS WERE SUPPOSEDLY MADE.

HOW DO YOU KNOW?

HAD SOME OLD CONTACTS IN THE SEX BUSINESS. THEY TELL ME SWEENEY HAD MORE THAN ONE FILM MADE HERE.

YOU FUCKING BASTARD, JERUSALEM.

YOU BRING THESE TWO GORGEOUS BITS OF STUFF HERE AND EXPECT ME TO TALK BUSINESS?

HOW MUCH TO GET 'EM TO PLAY TOGETHER WHILE WE JERK OFF OVER 'EM, eh? eh?

FUCKING GORGEOUS.

71

FILTHY ASSISTANTS, MEET MR. GRISHAM.

GRISHAM HAS BEEN THE CITY'S CHIEF PORNOGRAPHER FOR SOMETHING LIKE A HUNDRED AND FIFTY YEARS NOW.

NO ONE GETS OFF IN THIS TOWN WITH OUT HIM KNOW ABOUT IT.

AH, BUT YOU WANTED TO MEET ME OUT OF YOUR PROFOUND CONCERN FOR THE CONDITION OF POLITICS IN THE CITY TODAY. AND SO SOON AFTER THE ELECTION, TOO.

"DEMOCRACY IS THE THEORY THAT HOLDS THAT THE COMMON PEOPLE KNOW WHAT THEY WANT. AND DESERVE TO GET IT GOOD AND HARD."

MENCKEN.

AND, THANKS TO HIS ROGUE SECRETION-DWELLING NANOSENSORS, THAT IS LITERALLY TRUE IN OVER EIGHTEEN CITY DISTRICTS.

SO, IT OCCURRED TO ME, IF A CLEVER MAN REALLY WAS FUNDING PORNO WHILE TRYING TO FILIBUSTER SEX LEGISLATION OUT OF EXISTENCE, AND THAT GOT LEAKED--

I LEAKED IT. BECAUSE NO ONE ELSE WOULD KNOW SHIT ABOUT IT.

BUSTED. LET'S GO--

NO. THIS IS BACK-GROUND. STRICTLY OFF THE RECORD. THAT'S ALWAYS BEEN MY DEAL WITH GRISHAM.

WE HAVE JOURNALISTIC ETHICS, YELENA. PUT YOUR ATTACK WOMB AWAY.

MEET MELISSA. SHE LIVES IN THIS HOUSE. THIS IS THE BERLITZ-ABRAMS DISTRICT. THAT RING ANY BELLS, LADIES?

ROUND ABOUT THE TIME WHEN MELISSA HAD JUST GOTTEN OLD ENOUGH TO GET HERSELF DRINKS OF WATER FROM THE FAUCET, AN AUTONOMY-TERRORIST GROUP DROPPED INTELLECT SUPPRESSANT INTO THE WATER SUPPLY.

SHE'S NOT BRIGHT. SHE DOESN'T UNDER-STAND MUCH. SHE'S POOR AND SHE GETS FUCKED UP A LOT.

72

KNOW WHAT *THIS* IS?

IT'S A G-READER. READS GENOMES, HUNTS DOWN ROGUE SCRAPS OF GENETIC STRUCTURE, THAT SORT OF THING. THESE THINGS ONLY HIT THE STREETS A WEEK OR TWO BACK.

I DON'T KNOW WHAT EXACTLY WAS GOING ON HERE...BUT *SHE'S* GOT SCRAPS OF SWEENEY CLINGING TO HER.

AND SO DO YOU.

KNOW WHAT THE BEST THING ABOUT G-READERS IS?

ADMISSIBLE IN COURT.

AND SO'S THIS. VOICE RECORDING WITH GPS AND WORLD-CLOCK STAMP AND SEAL.

WHAT HAPPENED TO YOUR JOURNALISTIC ETHICS, YOU LITTLE MOTHERFUCKER?

THE *TRUTH,* GRISHAM. THAT'S ALL I NEED.

74

LONELY CITY

PRODUCED IN CONJUNCTION WITH THE TV SHOW

ESSAYS
SPONSORED BY
LONELY CITY™
TELEVISION

SPIDER JERUSALEM

Warren Ellis writes & Darick Robertson pencils
LONELY CITY
one of three

Rodney Ramos	Clem Robins	Nathan Eyring	Tony Harris	Ray Snyder	Cliff Chiang	Stuart Moore
Inker	Letterer	Color & Seps	Cover Pencils	Cover Inks	Ass't Editor	Editor

TRANSMETROPOLITAN created by Warren Ellis and Darick Robertson

Spider Jerusalem is the acclaimed columnist for the major metropolitan newspaper "The Word." These are essays from the doomed streets he haunts in pursuit of the Truth.

Channon Yarrow, a one-time stripper and convicted pay-dacoit, is Mr. Jerusalem's personal bodyguard and long-time confidante, providing protection during the writing of the "Lonely City" series.

Yelena Rossini, daughter of one of the city's oldest political families, is Mr. Jerusalem's personal assistant in both his daily life and his relentless hunt for the Truth.

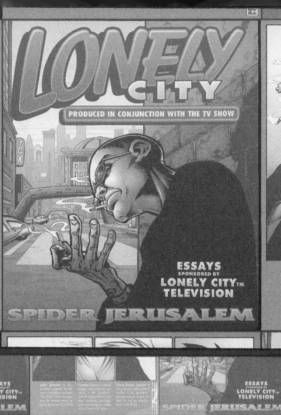

LONELY CITY

PRODUCED IN CONJUNCTION WITH THE TV SHOW

ESSAYS SPONSORED BY
LONELY CITY™ TELEVISION

SPIDER JERUSALEM

Spider Jerusalem is the acclaimed columnist for the major metropolitan newspaper "The Word." These are essays from the doomed streets he haunts in pursuit of the Truth.

Channon Yarrow, a one-time stripper and convicted pickpocket, is Mr. Jerusalem's personal bodyguard and long-time confidante, providing protection during the writing of the "Lonely City" series.

Yelena Rossini, daughter of one of the city's oldest political families, is Mr. Jerusalem's personal assistant in both his daily life and his relentless hunt for the Truth.

SPIDER JERUSALEM'S "LONELY CITY"

BOOKS·BOOKS

BOOKS

GENETIC STRUCTURE READER (COMMONLY: "G-READER") LEFT ON BODY OF RORY FLANAGAN LOCKWOOD, 17, KICKED TO DEATH BY FOUR ASSAILANTS JUST AFTER MIDNIGHT THIS MORNING.

LOCKWOOD'S GENETIC STRUCTURE CONTAINED THE CONTROVERSIAL CONCLAVE MODIFICATION, ALSO KNOWN AS THE POLY-TEMPLE OR SEXGANG CHANGE.

AH, HELL...

THE G-READER'S SCREEN STILL DISPLAYED ITS LAST SCAN--LOCKWOOD'S GENOME. ASSAILANTS SCANNED HIM PRIOR TO THE ATTACK.

I REMEMBER MY DAD KNEW A CLUTCH OF CONCLAVERS, WHEN I WAS A KID...

LOCKWOOD'S GENETIC SEQUENCE WAS ACTUALLY PRESENT IN ITS RECESSIVE, "DEAD" THIRD GENERATION ITERATION: NOT A DIFFERENCE THAT A CHEAP G-READER CAN DISTINGUISH.

CITY PD ARE LEAKING CASE DETAILS, AND WE EXPECT TO HAVE BUILT UP A PICTURE OF THIS KILLING AND THE CASE APPROACH BY TOMORROW MORNING

FUCK THAT!

FILTHY ASSISTANTS! SADDLE UP! ALL PROFESSIONAL APPARATUS ON; PREPARE TO HIT THE STREET!

I'M THE CLOSEST THING TO A REAL JOURNALIST *YOU'LL* EVER SEE, SHITEYES.

LETTING ME IN, OR SHALL I CALL AN AMFEED CREW TO TAPE ME BANGING ON THE DOOR?

ASSHOLE.

I'M DETECTIVE NEWTON. WHAT DO YOU *WANT*, JERUSALEM?

JUST CURIOUS.

LET'S GET ONE THING STRAIGHT HERE. I LIKE WHAT YOU DO. YOU HAVEN'T BEEN SERVED WELL BY THE POLICE. I WANT TO CHANGE THAT,

BUT IF ALL I'M DEALING WITH IS SOME DILETTANTE SON OF A BITCH WHO'S "JUST CURIOUS," YOUR ASS IS IN LOCOMOTION BACK TO WHATEVER STRIPCLUB YOU JACK OFF IN WHILE PRETENDING TO BE A WRITER.

"JUST CURIOUS" DOESN'T RATE INTRUSION INTO A CRIME SCENE. FIGURED YOU HAD MORE OF AN AGENDA THAN THAT.

AND WHAT HE HAD INSIDE, FROM HIS MOMMY AND DADDY AND GOD KNOWS WHO ELSE, IS THE GENETIC LEGACY OF A DESIGNED SUBSPECIES WITH MULTIPLE GENITALIA.

SEXGANG SEQUENCE. HIVED FAMILY STRUCTURES. CONCLAVER. AND THEY SCARED AND SICKENED PEOPLE, WAY BACK THEN.

THAT'S WHAT HE WAS KILLED FOR. THAT'S PERFECTLY CLEAR.

WHAT ISN'T CLEAR IS, YOU KNOW HOW MANY PEOPLE STOMPED HIM, BUT YOU'VE MADE NO ARRESTS, GIVEN NO DESCRIPTIONS, BEEN ECONOMICAL WITH YOUR LEAKS, AND SEQUESTERED THINGS PEOPLE SHOULD KNOW.

WHY HAVEN'T THE NEWSFEEDS PLAYED ANY OF THE DOZENS OF TAPES THAT SHOULD'VE BEEN MADE OF THIS?

IT'S A BUSY CITY STREET. MUST'VE BEEN A HUNDRED CAMERAS RUNNING HERE.

IT'S A BUS STOP. BUSES COME HERE. ANY BUS DEFENSE CAMERA ARRAY WOULD'VE PHOTOGRAPHED THE CORPSE WHEN IT PULLED UP HERE.

WHY ARE YOU SITTING ON THE TAPES, DETECTIVE NEWTON?

...OCKWOOD ...METHING.

YEAH, THE LOCKWOOD KID. COPS HAVE SNATCHED UP ALL CAMERA RECORDS OF THE INCIDENT.

AND?

AND **THEY** MUST KNOW WHO DID IT BY NOW. ODDS ARE PRETTY FUCKING GOOD THAT THOSE BASTARDS' FACES ARE ONSCREEN SOMEWHERE.

AND?

WHAT IS THIS, REMEDIAL DAY? DICKFUNGUS CRAWLED UP YOUR SPINE AND FILLED THE FRONT OF YOUR BRAIN WITH OOZE AND CHLOROPHYLL?

THEY'VE MADE NO ARRESTS.

THE COPS ARE GOING TO MAKE THIS GO **AWAY**. IT'S A MINORITY SLAYING AND THEY **DON'T** GIVE A SHIT.

DO YOU REALLY WANT TO FUCK WITH CPD AGAIN, SPIDER?

TRUTH?

NEW PRESIDENT!

NEW HOPE

Warren Ellis writes & Darick Robertson pencils

LONELY CITY
two of three

Rodney Ramos	Clem Robins	Nathan Eyring	Tony Harris	Jim Royal	Cliff Chiang
Inker	Letterer	Color & Seps	Cover Pencils	Cover Inks	Editor

TRANSMETROPOLITAN created by Warren Ellis and Darick Robertson

I jabbered and shrieked in the appalling chill of Dante Road, because I was naked and had been shot in the legs by sharpened ballistic popsicles. Strawberry and guava flavor. Fucking disgusting.

Winter apes jeered me from the park, jacking off with manic contempt, their futuristic innovation-packed semen crackling as it froze in the air mid-trajectory.

I found my bowel disruptor and made the noisy bastards shit themselves. They screamed, awful diarrheatic rushes instantly freezing into vile columns that pinned them to the ground by their bare, speckled asses.

Naked and severely wounded by a sociopathic ice cream salesperson. Obviously, the idea was that I'd awaken too weak to move, crippled, eventually to be slowly beaten to death by hails of frozen ape jizz.

My assistants were nowhere around, and I could see no cameras. So it wasn't them. Their attempts on my life are always characterized by recording equipment. They want to see me die and then play the video at a big party.

I WAS RESTING MY EYES.

WHAT DO YOU WANT?

CHECK THE TV NEWS.

WHAT'S THIS?

THIS IS THE PRECINCT HOUSE WHERE THE PEOPLE WHO KILLED LOCKWOOD ARE BEING HELD.

THEY ARRESTED THEM?

FINALLY, YEAH, AND IT LEAKED OUT THAT THEY WERE HERE.

BUT HALF OF THEM TURNED UP BEFORE THE ARRESTS, TO PROTEST THE COPS' LACK OF ACTION IN THE RORY FLANAGAN LOCKWOOD KILLING.

THIS MOB, THEREFORE, IS PRETTY MUCH YOUR FAULT, SPIDER.

THEY'VE GOT FANS.

THE PRESS, THE DEAD KID'S FAMILY AND FRIENDS, MINORITY RIGHTS GROUPS, OTHER SEXGANG PEOPLE.

SERVES 'EM FUCKING RIGHT.

ENGOGITO COOKIES

Better than that piss you're drinkin'!

Jason's 'GUN+FUN' hour click here

OLD PRECINCT

Life in Tuscany!

104

HOW DO YOU FEEL ABOUT THIS?

HM?

YOU ARE JOLT PROTECTED

HAVING THE COPS MOBBED. IT'S YOUR FAULT, YOU KNOW.

WE HAVE A PROBLEM, DON'T WE, YELENA?

YOU'RE A BIT OF A BELIEVER IN DUE PROCESS. A BELIEVER IN SOCIAL STRUCTURE AND AUTHORITIES DOING WHAT'S RIGHT.

TRADITION. LAW. PROBABLY COMES OUT OF YOUR FAMILY, THAT WHOLE PUBLIC SERVICE THING, RESPECT FOR THE LAW, SOCIAL FABRIC, ALL THAT.

SO, FROM YOUR VIEWPOINT, I'VE GOTTEN IN THE WAY OF THE COPS DOING THEIR VERY VERY IMPORTANT JOB.

AFTER ALL, THE COPS KNOW WHAT THEY'RE DOING.

LETTING PEOPLE DO THEIR JOB.

TARGET LOCKED

SPIDER JER

WHAT THE HELL ARE THEY REALLY DEMONSTRATING ABOUT, ANYWAY?

DO THEY NEED AN EXCUSE?

SPIDER GAVE THEM AN EXCUSE.

THEY'RE DEMONSTRATING BECAUSE THE POLICE TRIED TO SWEEP AWAY A MINORITY KILLING.

YOU DON'T KNOW THAT.

THEY HAVEN'T PRODUCED A DECENT EXPLANATION YET FOR HOLDING THE TAPES. AND IF THERE WAS A GOOD REASON--

AMFE

ICE
OR
WOOD

666

--THEN THE LIKES OF ME COULDN'T SHAME THEM INTO RELEASING THEM. THEY'D CONTINUE TO FOLLOW THAT PROCEDURE AND GIVE THAT AS THEIR EXPLANATION.

THEY FUCKED UP.

REMIND ME: I WANT COPIES OF THOSE TAPES.

THEY'VE LET THE FUCKERS OUT ON BAIL.

OUT ON BAIL, RELEASED OUT THE FRONT DOOR IN FRONT OF THE FUCKING MOB, ARMED COPS, SEALED AREA--

WHICH WAY?

I DON'T BELIEVE THIS SHIT--

I DON'T BELIEVE YOU CAME OUT UNARMED--

YOU KILLED MY SON YOU FUCKING **ASSHOLES!**

WE NEED TO GET THROUGH HERE.

NO ONE COMES THROUGH HERE, SIR. ORDERS.

WE WANT TO GET OUT OF HERE. WHY IS THAT A PROBLEM?

NO ONE GETS OUT OF THIS ENTIRE BLOCK. ORDERS WERE VERY CLEAR ON THAT.

WE'RE NO PART OF THIS. WE WANT NO PART OF THIS. WE WANT TO GET OUT.

PLEASE.

I'M SORRY, MISS.

NEXT TIME, GET A BETTER JOB.

AND A BETTER BOSS.

MOVE!

WHAT THE FUCK IS GOING ON, SPIDER?

THERE'S GOING TO BE A RIOT.

AND THE COPS ARE GOIN' TO LET IT HAPPEN.

GUNFIRE.

SETUP. THEY TURNED THE STREET INTO A KILLZONE AND WE WALKED INTO IT.

YELENA. THAT TRAIT YOU HAD. ARE *YOU* WIRED FOR PHONE?

YES. WHO DO YOU WANT?

ROYCE. THE WORD MUST HAVE A COMPLETE SET OF TAPES OF THE LOCKWOOD KILLING.

THERE'S MORE TO THIS THAN EMBARRASS-MENT. AND IT HAS TO BE ON THE SEQUESTERED TAPES.

SHIT SHIT SHIT--

ROYCE, IT'S YELENA ROSSINI--I NEED A READ ON THE LOCKWOOD TAPES THE POLICE RELEASED TODAY--GET THEM INTO A SMART SCANNER--

HEY--YOU'RE NOT ALLOWED DOWN HERE, YOU NEED TO BE BACK ON DANTE STREET--

Warren Ellis writes & Darick Robertson pencils

LONELY CITY

three of three

Rodney Ramos
Inker

Clem Robins
Letterer

Nathan Eyring
Color & Seps

Tony Harris
Cover Pencils

Drew Geraci
Cover Inks

Cliff Chiang
Editor

TRANSMETROPOLITAN created by Warren Ellis and Darick Robertson

...OKAY. ROYCE SAYS HE'S FOUND AN AMFEED RANDOM CAMERA INFECTION TRAVELING THE BREEZE DOWN THE STREET. SHOULD BE HEADED THE WAY WE WANT TO GO.

YELENA, I SEE ONE POLICE CAR, A PLASTIC BARRICADE. TWENTY FEET AROUND THE CORNER, MAYBE LESS.

TWO COPS IN THE CAR, ONE FIGURE WANDERING AROUND BEHIND, PROBABLY ON THE PHONE.

EVERYTHING'S GONE TO HELL HERE, YELENA. GET HOME.

TELL HIM TO BUY TIME ON IT, RIGHT NOW, AND PATCH THE IMAGERY TO HIS SCREEN.

THANKS, BOSS.

I'M YOUR BOSS, YOU DISLOYAL LITTLE TOAD.

SHUT UP. COP CAR RIGHT AROUND THE CORNER, TWENTY FEET OR LESS, BEHIND A LIGHT BARRICADE. TWO COPS INSIDE, ONE BEHIND.

RIGHT.

WHEN I SAY "RUN LIKE FUCK AND COMMIT ASSAULT ON A POLICE OFFICER SEVERAL TIMES," RUN LIKE FUCK AND COMMIT ASSAULT ON A POLICE OFFICER SEVERAL TIMES.

125

I NEED TO SANITIZE THIS LOCATION IMMEDIATELY.

MY BACK WAS TURNED SLIGHTLY TOO LONG TO SEE OR CATCH YOU.

DESK SERGEANT'S FAULT FOR DETAILING ME HERE BECAUSE HE'D RUN OUT OF WARM BODIES, WHICH IS WHY MY BACK WAS TURNED, RUNNING MY CASE-LOAD BY PHONE.

PATROL CARS HAVE A SPECIFIED EMP BURSTER THAT SHOULD KNOCK OUT THE CAMERAS IN THE VICINITY. OUGHT TO WIPE THEIR MEMORIES AND BUFFERS TOO.

ASSHOLES SHOULD'VE USED IT THE NIGHT LOCKWOOD GOT KILLED.

INSTEAD OF PLAYING WITH THE G-READER NEWLY INSTALLED IN ALL PATROL VEHICLES.

GET OUT OF HERE.

GO WRITE A STORY.

LEAVE ME OUT OF IT.

PURITAN MEWS
Residents Only

MAKER: TWO PERSONAL-RECIPE RESCUE RESTORATIVES, ONE SHOT OF BOURBON.

DRINK THESE DOWN SLOWLY.

WHAT IS IT?

I GOT TAUGHT HOW TO MAKE IT BY A SOLDIER IN BANGKOK WHOSE BASIC JOB WAS TO BE SHOT AT EVERY DAY. IT HELPS.

REMEMBER: A PARANOID IS SIMPLY SOMEONE IN POSSESSION OF ALL THE FACTS.

It's been a while since anyone tried to kill me.

A little less than two hours ago, CPD tried to silence the critics of their handling of the Lockwood case in a fairly original manner. They rounded them up and shot them. At this point, I have no idea how many casualties there are. I don't have time for that.

Because you need to know, now, that CPD have finally come unglued. They cannot survive this act of ultimate brutality. We cannot let them survive it.

STORY'S DONE AND SENT.

JUST IN TIME. TV NEWS FINALLY GOT SOME CAMERAS INTO DANTE STREET.

WITH THE CORDON AROUND DANTE STREET PRECINCT HOUSE LIFTED, THE SCENE THAT AWAITS US IS ONE OF CARNAGE AND LOSS...

SINCE WHAT CPD CLAIMS WAS A TERRORIST ACTUATION OF AN ELECTROMAGNETIC PULSE BURSTER KILLED EVERY CAMERA IN THE VICINITY, THERE IS NO FOOTAGE OF THE ACTUAL EVENTS.

constant NEWS

ON YOUR SCREENS NOW: RORY LOCKWOOD'S MOTHER. LOCKWOOD'S ENTIRE FAMILY, GATHERED HERE TODAY TO PROTEST, HAVE BEEN CONFIRMED DEAD.

THE OFFICIAL POLICE STATEMENT POINTS TO AGITATORS WITHIN THE LOCKWOODS' GROUP OF WELL-WISHERS AS THE CAUSE OF THIS HORROR.

ROUNDED US ALL UP INTO ONE PLACE AND KILLED US.

PHONE. IT'S ROYCE. I'LL TRANSFER YOU TO THE HOUSE PHONE.

ROYCE? NOW DON'T YOU DARE ASK ME WHERE YOUR FUCKING COLUMN IS, YOU SON OF A BITCH, I JUST SENT YOU A MOTHERFUCKER OF A PIECE...

WHAT?

CALLAHAN.